CW00828166

THE CITY OF EXETER
and the Exe Valley

Photographs by Bob Croxford

Exeter, and the valley of the River Exe, is one of the most fertile areas in England. The ancient Celts called the river Isca, or water. The Romans came to this spot nearly 2,000 years ago and established a town, in a commanding position by a crossing of the river, and called it Isca Dumnoniorum. The bishopric of Crediton moved to Exeter and established the cathedral in 1050.

Many of the pictures in this, and other Atmosphere books, are available as large photo prints to fram For details of sizes and prices please see www.atmosphere.co.uk/prints.html

Published by Atmosphere
Willis Vean
Mullion Cornwall TR12 7DF
England
Tel 01326 240180
email info@atmosphere.co.uk

ISBN 0 9543409 6 5

Printed and bound in Italy

Frontispiece   EXETER CATHED

Bishop Branscombe began the building of a grandiose new CATHEDRAL in 1

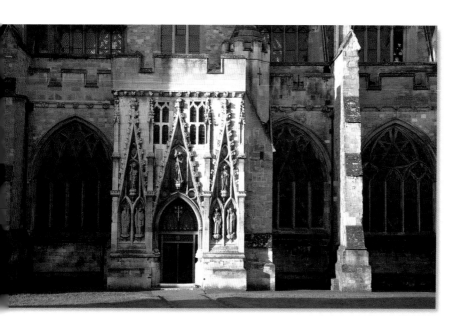

Statue of RICHARD HOOKER, the Exeter di

EXETER CATHEDRAL, built in Decorated Gothic style THE CATHEDRAL at n

Through an archway to the BISHOP OF CREDITON'S HO

timber-framed MOL'S COFFEE HOUSE was built in 1596   A sweep of Tudor Cottages, Cathedral Close

Mural of PRINCESS HENRIETTE ANNE (daughter of Charles I and born in Exeter), High S

...ess steel spheres form part of Michael Fairfax's EXETER RIDDLES sculpture

The Norman Gatehouse leads to EXETER CAS

old CROWN COURT HOUSE

THE SHIP INN, an old haunt of Sir Francis Drake's   THE 15th century GUILDH

The 900 year old ceremony of Proclaiming LAMMAS FAIR, in mid June each year, is a colourful affair. A decorated white glove is paraded through the streets in a procession of school children and dignatories. The Right Worshipful The Lord Mayor of Exeter and Honorary Alderman travel in the former Sheriff's horse drawn coach and are announced by the Town Crier and flanked by a pair of Mace Sergeants. The proclamation is made outside the Guildhall after which the glove, which symbolises Royal protection, is hoisted above the street for the three day duration of the Fair.

THE QUAYSIDE area is a charming mix of past and present

The 17th century CUSTOM HOUSE is located on historic Quay

CUSTOM HOUSE was an important part of Exeter's colourful maritime past

THE PROSPECT INN and old CUSTOM HOUSE   THE QUAYSIDE area at night·

An iron footbridge crosses the lane to CATHEDRAL GR

YSIDE FOOTBRIDGE spans the RIVER EXE on Exeter's waterfront

The MEDIEVAL EXE BRIDGE is the oldest surviving in Britain

The MILLER'S CROSSING BRIDGE and its mill wheel fe

SOUTHERNHAY, lined with fine Georgian townhouses, is the heart of the commercial di

...eria climbs over an elegant office in SOUTHERNHAY

Dawn in the Devonshire countryside near Powderham C

The view from HALDON RIDGE.

The triangular castle HALDON BELVEDERE was built high on Haldon Hill in

boats on the River Exe Estuary, TOPSHAM

Reflections at TOPSHAM

LYMPSTONE, one of Devon's prettiest villages, framed by red sandstone cliffs   A fishing boat sails the Exe Estuary near EXMO

On the signpost:

EXMINSTER 2½
KENTON 3
KENNFORD 1

Exeter 5
Chudleigh 8
N.Abbot 11

Traditional country pub in KENN

TURF LOCK where the River Exe meets the Exeter

The Collegiate Church of the Holy Cross at CRED

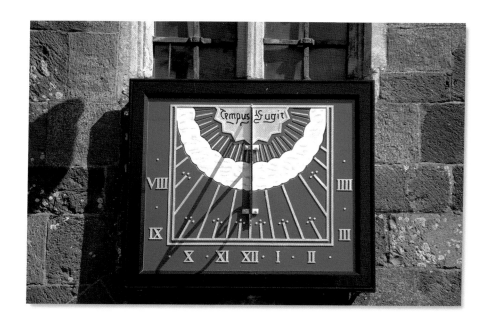

A peaceful churchyard in the centre of CREDI

busy market town of TIVERTON stands on the Rivers Exe and Lowman

BICKLEIGH is a charming village in the Exe

The famous iron-rich red soil of East Devon is very f

INDEX

Leaf: The RIVER EXE upstream from Exeter